# You Are Meant to Be Like Fire

Sheila Murray-Nellis

Thank you to the editors where some of these poems have previously appeared:

"When the Wheel Turns" won first prize in the 2012 Kootenay Literary Competition and appears in their anthology *Revolution;*

"The Taste of the Wind," "What's Beneath The Surface," "The Moon Wouldn't Let the Sky Be Dark," "The Distant Wind," "While Alone, Thoughts Escape," and "Tangled" were all part of the first prize entry of the 2010 Kootenay Literary Competition and appear in their anthology *When Words Take Flight,* and "The Taste of the Wind," "What's Beneath The Surface," and "Tangled" also appear in the online journal *Clarion;*

*St. Katherine Review:* "Invisible Highway";

*Mslexia:* "Lumberjack Transformed";

*In Our Midst:* "Ripples."

**Cover illustration by Janet Walker**

**Eva Nova Press**
**P.O. Box 313**
**Kaslo, BC**
**V0G 1M0**
**Canada**

For Robert, who has shared the joys and the struggles.

These poems are a selection from three main parts of my life corresponding to three places I have lived: Harrington, Quebec, where my husband and I raised our three sons and a flock of sheep on the farm owned by Charles and Alba Taylor; Pomfret, Vermont, where our sons went to school; and Birchdale, BC, where we are building a Byzantine-style chapel from stone.

# Contents

## Crossing the Lake

"The whole earth is a living icon of the face of God."
St John of Damascus


"Beauty will save the world."
*The Idiot* by F. Dostoevsky

# Harrington, Quebec: Slicing Silence

# Ripples

I stand, washing dishes and feeling the years
gurgling as they circumnavigate the drain;
the present gapes from the center, noisily sucks up my life.

Outside, behind a screen of saplings,
a deer walks gingerly at the edge of the wood,
stops, and sniffs the air;

a black crow perches on the branch of a tree
whose crabapples glisten like rubies; he calls
to his cronies who, fluttering black, cluster among the limbs.

And I am here.
I fling open the door, traipse through the dewy grass,
my socks wet and a damp wind slipping beneath my collar.

Why do I stay? It has to do with the way
weather comes in waves: first, sunlight bathes the hills
like laughter, the autumn trees shine golden light,

and the dew on the grass sparkles; then purple clouds
glide across the sky sprinkling rain. Minutes later,
hail patters the ground and there are a few wet flakes of snow.

Suddenly the clouds are gone, the sky is blue,
but you can see the hail still slashing the valley
and the rippling of the storm over the landscape.

# There's a Purple About November

It's in the barks of trees, the slabs of granite
hugging the road, and the underbelly of clouds,
a swirling purple that melts into burnt sienna.

October's orange and yellow and scarlet
have slipped off
and the empty branches blush

curving with a November shiver;
sumac berries, once scarlet,
now whither into burgundy and brown.

Soon purple enters my bones
and lodges in my memory,
a purple like the river's curves

that turns my mind side to side,
an ambling beast making for home,
the purple of silence and sadness

and a tormenting thirst.
There's a longing about November,
a yearning towards mystery;

it comes with the honking of geese
and the bite of a cold breeze,
the desire to be alone, yet not alone,
a longing for home.

# Lumberjack Transformed

All that winter you slogged through hip-deep snow
with your chainsaw, shovel, half a dozen
peanut butter sandwiches and wearing

a yellow hard hat, plaid jacket, steel toe
boots, and padded pants. You'd come home again
after dark, aching muscles and smelling

of gas and spruce pitch. The night Frankie Doe
came with you, I met you at the gate. Then
Frankie cawed and squawked to the gathering

black winged clustering clouds until the crows
cawed back. He lifted his arms and flapped in
frenzied circles. They flapped back. Then lifting,

he sailed through the air, and we watched him go,
his flailing black hair tapered to resin
feathers. We still stand here skyward watching.

# On This Crisp Morning

Frost ices the shadows
by the aspen's feet,

dew spits on the grass
while sunlight keeps

pouring, pouring
from a pitcher of blue.

# The Sun, a Grape

on the horizon's
pink tongue,
squirts its wine
across the white
expanse.

Intoxicated, I
watch the opening
of a billion eyes
as I plunge
through the meadow's
crust, knee deep;
snow seeps
down my boots,
the sweet
smell of wet wool.

Now I plunge
and now
perch on the surface
stretched
wafer thin;
I'm breathless
hushed
until my teeth echo
the sound of
collapsing crust.

# Moose Chase in Fog

*(for Aaron)*

If fog swallows the memory of what's now hidden,
if when you look outside your window,
instead of the old apple tree and lilac bush,

milky air advances and recedes
in a teasing dance,
would it surprise you to see

four lanky legs beneath the white
and later a head nibbling the plastic strap
of a ski pole stuck into the crusty snow—

would you follow the gangly escape
into white oblivion, or would you
bound after that shining boy

who cannot hold back, who
plunges through fog in pursuit, unable to see
ahead but moving arms and legs through a sea

of white; would you not follow then,
although you can't keep up,
although you fear your footing is awkward and slow,

would you keep stepping
would you dance even when your legs fail
would you dance on your elbows into white light?

# How St. Francis Sings

Teach always
and if necessary
use words;
then he leapt over
Italian meadows
brown cloak
flapping like bird
wings.

Hold life in a cup
of light
fellow creature
fellow crooner
fellow joy bellower!

Don't you know
these we
name
turn moist eyes
on us,
chewing cuds
of expectation,
preening feathers
of mercy?

See how their flight
parts to the right
and to the left;

See how your own heart
lifts her wondrous wings!

19

# Lamb

Hooves click on linoleum;
          wriggling tail taps the tumbled
down cardboard box; traces of
milk replacer powder dust
          the counter; and out comes one
          green beer bottle with plastic
nipple dribbling white; the small

black wrinkled body nipping
          my pant leg, his thin bleat is
nipping my heart. Why he's here
is his mother gave birth in
          a blizzard and his wet wool
iced up; we gathered him in
close to the stove. Then the ewe

forgot, snubbed him, so he's ours.
          Back in the barn, he is first
to greet us, hooves propped against
the dutch door, he bleats stronger
          now, sure we'll offer him milk.
When we let the flock into
the meadow the lamb hangs back.

Lingering with children who
        pat castles in sand, he bleats
and sucks on their plump fingers.
Once named he's no one's dinner;
        he'll be fed hay; yearly he'll
offer wool. "You're a fool," says
my neighbor. "But listen," I

reply. The children squeal when
        he leaps in the meadow, his
back legs spring sideways; naming,
then, is how we learn to see.
        Naming, we learn to speak rock's
compact denseness and the lace
when ferns flicker shade just so.

These we gather when we stand
        in worship; these we offer
through the lamb to his delight
that we notice the joy formed.

# Blue Night

and orange crescent moon
rising between the purple hills;
wind, the color of hope
whipping from the east
rattles the windows' loose teeth.

I hold my cup of blue night
steaming, the color of dreams
warming the silence;
you and I the color of dancing,
the shadows are liquid and long.

# Summer

Sheep clump
under the maple for shade;

thistles rise by cowpies,
yarrow and daisies
        and purple vetch;

puffy cumulous
in the blue sky,
cicadas buzz
after a long stretch of dry;

basswood leaves rustle,
the jays of midday,
a distant rumbling tractor
cutting hay.

# The Distant Wind

It's because of the flatness all about, beyond these green hills
that bulge up along the thrashing river,

It's because of the distant flatness and the way
the wild wind whips past that brings this hissing in the trees,

This constant motion, that lifts the turkey vultures,
that brings the rumbling thunder, that makes

Trees fall broken-hearted, trees that had once sprung up
curving their roots around and under solid granite.

It's because of the song that lifts through my larynx,
the wind that enters the flow of wind,

And where this wind comes from and where it goes,
singing notes that called into being these very notes within.

It's because of the sweet motion of the river that lifts up
singing through the wind's song with its own rushing

And that of the sea to which it flows.
I wait below. If you hear me sing you'll know

It's not my song alone: I'm singing the wind;
I'm singing the sound of the waters;

I'm singing the way home.

## To You Who Lives There Now

Have you taken the path yet
out past the house
and over the ledge on the north side
                    of the barn
where the mother killdeer feigns a broken
wing to lure you from her little brown eggs
                    laid in a cup of rock?
Go through the gate on the broken rail fence
                    overgrown with hawthorn
along the grassy trail, past boulders
into the green lace of cedar branches.
Squirrels will chitter a warning as you approach—
                    Ignore that.
Veer to the right and you will come
to the spongy moss speckled red
                    open to the sky.
Cedars huddle around the edges.
Fall on your face there—
                    listen
to what the breeze says.
You are meant to bear
that kind of light.

# New England Poems: The Long Longing

# What's Beneath The Surface

If you were someday
to rise out of the foaming waters of the sea
to count the stones and broken shells of my heart,

If you were to listen there
and to separate the gull's cry
from the sucking sounds of stones beneath inhaling waves,

If only you were there at night
when shivering stars gaze with longing,
if you added your breath to the wind that tangles my hair

And strokes my neck with cold fingers,
then you would lift the pebbles to expose the sand
ground to softness by weather.

Once home in your room
you would put the spiraled shell to your ear
and listen to my whispered lament.

You would unwind the ribbon of kelp
from your heart and reveal the cords
that bind it to my own.

# Beach In December

When we saw the sky seep beneath the Isles of Shoals
     and saw them levitate,
when the sea swells stained pastel like old church windows
     and kelp echoed the foam's curve,
then the sea spit stones on the sand
     beside the gull-smashed crab shell
     amidst the putrid smell of rotting fish—
that's when the cancer returned to gnaw my father's bones.

When I was small, we walked the beach together
     picking jewel-colored glass from among the stones,
their sharp edges worn down by waves and time
     and their colors salted creamy white.
We said we would put them by the window
     where they would catch the light,
but later we'd find them in our pockets
     or dumped from a sand pail
in the grass behind the cottage.

My father sucked in his opinions like stones
     and spit them out again,
the way his snores rumbled the house
     or the television droned on,
blue light flickering over his features
     becoming one with his eyes
whose light clouded over
     sea storm hazel.

We always heard the waves in the distance.

His war ship's splattered deck
        called him back before his death
to wander there among the ghosts
        and in the wandering
brought his own ending close.

We sat by his bed on Christmas Eve
        too late to bring up our own wars
that follow us still, sucking our strength
        stoning us as we sit by the waves,
time smoothing what's left.

We still walk the shore where my father sat in his beach chair
        looking out at those isles on the horizon.
They flicker in and out of our vision
        depending upon the weather, the fog,
and then just when cold's claws reach out to clutch them,
        they rise.

# American Tourist

On narrow Irish roads
where an inopportune sneeze
would etch your form on a storefront
or a seaside cliff,
where drowsy sheep warm damp wool
on the pavement, unflinching
as you inch past
moss-furred famine houses
that crumble into the bog;
black turf cut from earth
in chunks stooked up to dry
will later be gathered to burn.
Do the ghosts return?
Or are we, born abroad,
those ghosts who see our faces
in those we pass in the villages,
we unconnected ones
with an Irish name, freckled skin,
sucking in sounds
whispered in a childhood home,
a sadness in a grandmother's eyes,
memories we don't remember
but that claim us just the same
with the binding that ties
us to just this place
we see now for the first time.

# Just Beyond

The brook carves the field,
meanders, then slithers
into the forest
where water bubbles
over stones that jut
their chins, the spray's
downy beard hangs in air,
and this moment opens.

When you take a breath
        here by the brook, breathe
burst bubbles, breathe
the rising air,
breathe my breath, as I
breathe yours,
and we sail upwards,
each other's lungs
filling with gurgles of promise
within clutch
of ribs.

I have rooted
myself in your heart,
I have rooted myself,
stretched past
what wraps me up
with strips of thought,
the stone rolled
by light.

# Musings by a Vermont Pond

Blue heron picks
through still water, makes
no ruffle, on stick
legs, mist wafts across, takes

its time, his needle beak
knits through gilded grass on shore;
a gibbous moon above the willow,
hundreds of geese settle, then shift some more

in the field cleared of hay,
their cries like the despairing multitudes;
you sit in a dusty city, while a Vermont pond
ripples from your breath its solitude;

did you forget the gibbous moon
blinking its silver eye, paled in a wash of blue,
but hanging there nevertheless?
I picked through old boxes of you,

blowing dust from photos, rereading the letters
of memory as of a nagging hindsight.
Somewhere there's a pile of you dumped in a back room
cascading onto the floor of the nights

I waited alone for morning;
if only you had left a fragment alive,
a single volume not ravaged by mice,
a whiff of you might have survived

leaving, as it's time
to go the way geese will go
when the picking's no longer good,
insects dead or buried under the snow.

# Tangled

We found the finch,
eyes clear but wings
limp as string,
its spindly feet
twisted in wire.

Untangling toes,
you were quick to stroke
ruffled feathers;
then you hung back:
the small body
fluttered to the oak.

You wear your fatigue
like feathers; I stretch
out my hand; your feet
lock in to what snares
you even more.

With your every twist
my heart is pierced
with barbs.

## Veneer

Politeness covers her heart so you can't get close.
I'm in despair, vulnerable
as a peeled egg,

thoroughly ridiculous,
my unwashed shirt and my smile
equally wrinkled.

# Warming

Winter is late this year
and the clouds' gray fists ripple
across a windy sky
where birds flock
squawking
in a swirling ball of wings.

The lip of moon slips
over the meadow's crease
surprises us, unprepared
even on these abbreviated days
as does this warm December air
in Vermont, where the snow

has usually capped the hills by now
and frost iced the fields,
yet here we are
balmy winds rattling Christmas lights
against the Chase's plastic Santa,
and though we brag to each other
about our thin sweaters,

what we really feel is an eerie unease
that spreads over our necks
instead of mufflers
as we tell about the bulbs
sprouting across the river
and the pair of sparrows
lining their nests
with milkweed fluff.

## Swollen Desire

The black horizon
drifts closer,
explodes over our heads
pulsing light, rumbling,
pelting us with rain, with hail,
pricking our skin, and then
the slithering cloud
settles as if on eggs,
smothers us with its dark feathers,
while each of us thinks only of our own bowels,
a constipation of nerve.

If we read this in a history book, we would ask
Why did those people say nothing?
Why did they let more
        and again
more slip by
rumbling as it was
the icy words pricking their skin?

But then, this is now
and so we shrug, imagining
this will pass
        —it is only angels bowling
or the rumbling of a giant's belly,

and we turn again to our own bellies
swelling with gas.

# This Long Longing

       is for more than a pocket
or even a home;

We pierce through to the kingdom
then trip on the threshold.

On the edge of that meeting place,
face embracing face,
we sit side by side, beyond
       rivalry, beyond pride;

If you fall asleep, I will protect you;
I'll keep your head from drooping,
smooth the lock of hair from your brow.

To reach your hand, I stretch past
the pool that cups my tears—
       swimming there for days on end
has made me dizzy, but if
I grasp your hand and focus on your eyes,
         I can leap
over the place that sucks me in.

I turn my heart inside
out, seeking that lost coin—
this long and wrenching turning.

My hair is gray with longing,
your touch evaporates—
here I sit in hope's envelope, sad
for the wildness that even now
casts me both away
                    and recklessly into
    the fires of such
            dauntless love—

    this long and wrenching turning

## Between

Sometimes when I look up at the sky,
one cumulus cloud slips by another
beneath the wispy cirrus high above,

and suddenly the sky as a ceiling opens up
and there's an awesome feeling of space and depth,
and then I look at you

and I see more than I see,
the space that is invisible between us
becoming somehow visible,

and the tiny box I have built up around my heart explodes,
and there we are, more than you
and more than myself, a between somehow existing

not in itself, but in the coming together of the two,
and I know I have stepped into this fullness
more profound than life itself

a space not empty but teeming with presence
and energy, and all those
I have ever loved are there

as are you; I can tell from your eyes
you have seen it, too,
and though we may never speak of it—

for what, in fact, can one say at all?
—together we have stood in that between
where life

 even beyond death
is truly victorious.

## Icicles

Warm wind in deep December,
snow softens on the dune;
like teeth at my window casement,
the icicles drip the moon.

Moon soft upon the meadow,
her unction brings a glow,
and now the wind will join the sound
as our voices sing below.

The entrance of the very life
that holds us in embrace,
and all the earth in wonder:
fiery summer, frosty lace.

## Amaryllis

I'm sitting waiting for this amaryllis to open
—could be a long wait.
Look at these five ruby-tipped stamens
on the flower already unfurled,
yellow pistils like corkscrew curls,
drops of dew waiting to roll over petals

open for only a day before they drop;
new buds like praying fingers
suddenly open; just since
we've been sitting here, this one
has started to loosen;
I'm watching till it unfolds.

When the breeze tosses them like that
they're agreeing with some silent wisdom,
and then they do that loosening thing
till pretty soon the dew drips
        from their center to the petal tips.
I've never seen one open.

# Mother Sea

The sea's hushing, the sea's
ceaseless shushing
        the cares of the wind
lapping up continents and whipping
spume from the expanse of sea;

you'd think the sea would grow tired,
but through the night's yawn
and through the day's tedious gaze
on she rocks and croons her lullabies.

The thing about the sea is
she keeps coming
        even in the rain, she follows upon herself
wave after wave, and the sound of her
        and the smell
        and the way she keeps on
until inside you somewhere you can hear her
in the place between waking and sleep;
your mind fills with the rush
        and the chill up your legs
        and the breath at your neck.
She sucks you into herself with the same long thirst
that she drinks in pebbles from the shore
        and then she pushes you back
and the power and the expanse
all her waves and billows
cover me.

Sea's hunger grows
nuzzles the shore, then licks
     and sputters, now bounds
guzzling like a colt
sucks her saliva through stone teeth
spits back again, higher each time,
eager to be loosed from her tether.

The surprise of moon smoothing sea
with silvery fingers at night
and in the day, the sky's blue skin.
     You reach out to touch it,
but your hand pushes right through—
nothing solid at all—
the white clouds mimic
the shape of the hills
     though if you were to lean there
you'd tumble backwards.

Why do we watch the shore
studying the horizon—
     waiting for a ship, perhaps?
or someone frantically riding in the waves
bearing a message:

the loosed colt,
spread shawls over puddles,
screaming stones.

# Birchdale Poems: Crossing the Lake

# The Taste of the Wind

*(a haiku sequence)*

Milk in a tin can
Your voices softly argue
Moonlight floods the snow.

The moon's melon slice
From the bowl's indigo rim
Seeps a bleeding yolk.

Timid steps at dawn
Beneath the rumpled blankets
Parents softly snore.

In a white kitchen,
Three bowls of dreaming people
The silence of dawn.

An orange squirtsjuice,
Dried egg between the fork's prongs
Your breakfast farewell.

Fog before my eyes,
Your voice like tiny scissors
Through the paper storm.

Wet by the shore's edge
The memory still lingers,
Pebbles cupped in rock.

Weak voice on phone line
I hear you slipping from me
Chimney smoke shadow.

Pen slips from my grip
Trace words with moistened fingers
Words vanish in air.

I wait in silence,
Shabby couch and smoke-stained walls
Dust collects in tufts.

Lone fir in moonlight
Long years I listen for you
Still the waves suck stones.

The pines remember
Your whisper on a cold night
The taste of the wind.

# Wandering Through the Light Cast

by swirling snow or at least
my gaze is wandering past
the glass and out to the feast

of silhouettes where
deer toe through fluff;
is it enough to see my own construction
when through the window over tufts

the prickly branches twig my sight;
needles scratch on up the mountain
to hang on clouds that leak light.
Through glass I observe and defer;

deferring, I judge and hold back
what could be life, until holding
back is habitual, is the life I hack
and discuss and deconstruct.

How can I
recede into myself when hence
Life evaporates drop by drop

instead of slaking thirst?

# Deer's Cloven Prints

A silent presence
imprinted on snow,

cold the way a word is cold
as it passes from you to me,

or more often still,
is muffled in the space between us

where even your breath
has vanished

and the snow holds no memory
of your footprints.

# December 20th, 2010

*Alignment of the Full Moon, Solstice, and Lunar Eclipse*

Alone here in the moonlight
I think of your silence and wonder

how the glisten of moon on snow
can tell me something I may have forgotten

to say, or perhaps a thought that was
crystal clear to me

froze as it passed between us
and made your beauty sink

the way the stones on the road
duck when the frost pushes up.

I can see the colors in the frosty ground
as light is bent by snow.

Your colors still shine
even now on the darkest night of the year.

# The Moon Wouldn't Let The Sky Be Dark

You were the one whose name I heard
when the wind moved through the valley.

I heard the trees whisper it, but
you weren't listening at the time.

The moon kept pouring more and more
silver into the sleeping lake.

I saw your eyes snap open:
That's when you began to shimmer.

See how the waters wait for your voice's ripple.
See how the still waters shine.

# Crossing the Lake at Night

We hear the rolling waves,
the snap of the flag,
but still we step
into the aluminum boat
settle on the bench,
and ease from the dock
into the black night.

The pitch of the waves,
wild beasts beneath us
we cannot see but feel,
erupt now here, now
            there
as if a hundred fishes
carry us in their rollicking play.

If it were day,
we would see the white caps;
we would know this wind
whirls from the south,
but in the dark
the mouth with all the teeth
nips our faces,
tears at the boat,
and we cry out,
and we lock eyes,
and then the sudden calm
and then the still.

# A Different Kind of Knowledge

Moor the boat,
clip the rope to the chain
slimy beneath the water,
pull it up hand over hand,
the buoy slippery
with brown scum,
its top bobbing on the ripples;

silvery morning spills
on the waters, fish
fins beneath the satin;
the steely sky
has plump clouds;
in a flash of eyes
thoughts crack the sky.

What I'm trying to
say is all about your
silver and the ways
that slip beneath us,
fuzzy beneath the surface,
slipping through
our naked hands;

what we strive to create
evades our grasp,
a fish teasing as it leaps,
then a liquid slither;
moor the boat,
clip the rope to the chain
of happenings

slimy all about us,
then climb onto the dock,
step on solid ground again;
the walk along the tree-lined
path will steady you,
your weary steps sheltered
beneath the cedar branches.

# Invisible Highway

The moose traveled the same invisible highway
we saw the buck deer go:

First the splash
then antlers bobbing above the waves;

the frigid lake buoys them
to the far shore where they scramble

onto the pebble beach by Clute Creek,
pick their way through the cedars

where the logging road leads up
to St. Mary's Wilderness Park.
It's the same route every time.

I step into my boat,

the lake slick, then stirred.

Already I drift
from the dock, the cliffs
stark, sheer to the bottom,

this pallet of doubt
my door.

I'm here where others
have gone before

through lashing waters
that churn and masticate.

Across the lake
a voice parts the waves

breathes through
wind and thrashing hooves
and I come to the shore

where wilderness leads to the core
on high and windy mountains.

I listen: the ice melts
above the sprouting meadows
and its trickle
overflows the tarn.

# The Hidden Cave

Christmas afternoon
and we are walking the wooded path
to South Beach;
we find cougar tracks
weaving down from the mountain
through the stand of ponderosa
pine to the lake's edge.

We follow to their source
up the ridge, in and out
of boulder piles and along a fallen trunk;
we trace the snow dimpling of squirrels
and the mouse highways between a log
and some stones and how
a coyote sniffed its edges.

The day after the night when the animals speak,
we learn of their trails over snow,
writing their movements across the paths we walk,
and when we stop to sing the typika,
our voices drift over the treetops
and ruffle the waters of the lake
while animals huddle in the deep woods

and listen to what our ears no longer hear:
angel voices echoing against the mountain,
leaving their prints where they've danced through
air, rattling crystal branches tinkling to the ground.

Hark!—their voices spin the electrons in the air molecules;
Hark!—someone whimpers in the cave
          we pass without bothering to enter;
Hark!—even our denials lead us to the edge.

# On Theophany Eve

*I.*

Slip sliding on the dock
on Theophany eve,
we yank in the boat,
enter, and wipe snow from the dash;

    my bare hands unmoor the bow,
yours the stern;
pushed by waves the fuel line ices,
the engine stalls;
you add antifreeze to the tank
and work it through by squeezing the bulb;
I row to keep us in place;
waves nudge us to the pebbly shore,
the rocky cliffs,
all my effort just to keep steady;

    for fear of shallow waters, I lift the engine;
your breath steams as your working hands
pop crystals in the rubber;

an hour on the waves
before the engine catches.

Nothing stays intact:
a constant roll of water;
the wind,
waves rock me;
the swell, the unsettling
persistent wavering;
life's movement,
everything on the brink,
each breakthrough a miracle;
keeping steady

        our hands,
        the rocks,
        the oars.

*II.*

When His head went under the water,
who could have predicted the rumbling up
as molecules rearranged themselves in His light?

It was as if a rupture in the fabric of the world
let in eternity's ocean,
at first, drop by drop,
then in a stream,
finally bursting through the threads
of time that tried so hard to restrain
such powerful persistence,
a whoosh of wave.

*III.*

Once Life has been baptized, what then?
Once Love submerges into the flowing river,
how can the waters maintain their separate stance?

Each molecule of space and time
soaked in Love
while the Father's voice repeats,
"I am pleased. I am well
pleased. Good,
        it is very good."
Wings brood over the depths.

Catch me up, breathe on these hands
I've let grow cold, pulling on oars,
the wood keeping us on course,
and I'll follow you into the waves, then
re-emerge, be
caught up by flight.

## Waters

The waters bear
your ribbon of life
and all the worlds you have borne,

your blood and the movement of your dreams,
the way you dreamt them and how
you molded them in the telling.

The waters buoy them now,
reflect the heights they yearn for,
transposed from here to there

on the depths,
the glacial streams that feed the source,
the sky and all it holds.

# In My Boat

Beams
slash through clouds,
leak a golden puddle;

a fishing boat passes through it,
the people in silhouette;
I am less translucent than I should be.

The light approaches:
I must empty my boat,
offer my stones,

see them sparkle.

# When I Lingered in the Garden

A crash in the woods,
deer rush through the trees:
it's probably a black bear
down from the mountain.

I keep pulling roots from the soil.
I've just planted the small Russian potatoes,
all full of eyes, saved from the root cellar,
and the quack grass worms
its long roots along the beds,
seeking water.

I stand and clear my throat;
black
        against the white birch—
he is beautiful
yet strong and unpredictable.
He looks up, startled enough
to scoot beside the tree but
        not enough to leave.

He looms between the garden and the house.

I speak gently to him
as I ease
towards the cabin
on the far side of the garden

where I sit now;
the chimney needs cleaning,
and the stove will not hold a fire
this crisp day in May
as ants trail across the porch.

I, too, yearn for living waters
and come down from my lofty hideaway.
I crash through
the forest at the foot of the mountain.
Take me over where the deer wander,
so I thirst for thee
so I thirst.

# While Alone, Thoughts Escape

The sky is mulling over its thoughts.

She has more teeth than she needs for chewing;
her lips struggle to keep them in;
their yellow bite drains the white
of her eyes and muddies the grey roots
of her hair. Somewhere she has set
her glasses if only she could remember
if only she could focus her mind:
this kind of trouble becomes more familiar;
it would be funny except for the wasted time.

Her thoughts are over the sky, mulling.

She spirals up the logging road,
paintbrush blush on the banks, black
spruce needle the mountain's back.
Up here trees sift the wind,
raven wing feathers whine in reply;
a creek bubbles over stones,
fists of clouds loosen
then make shadow puppets

on the hill's screen.
See where the mountain gave way,
tumbled in a mess of stones, and how
the moss reclaims it for the trees.

She reclaims her thoughts tumbling
over and under the clouds
like cumulus that darken,
become nimbus,
roll with rumbling,
spark with light, bright
thoughts with darker underbellies,
dark thoughts that crack
their shells and drop their raw suns
into the bowl the hills make.

# Crows

Crows gather on snow
their black beaks peck
the ice that coats
the walks, the road.

Below the surface,
pebbles and a splash of blood
where the deer misjudged
the fender of the speeders;

now the garrulous cleaners
peck while carrying on
their cryptic conversation,
interrupted in a flutter

when we inch along
the slick, new dusted street;
shadows cover
their soiled feathers,

disguise their three-
toed steps,
while we speak of betrayals
and watch the white road
stain red.

# To Know Evil Is to Know the Distance

It sits on the tongue like the sweetest fruit,
pinches with bitter aftertaste,
and gradually numbs the mouth;

the paralysis creeps
until how to turn back slips from memory;

bolting becomes habit,
as if you could get anywhere
through separation.

I watch the footprints pressing the snow
but seldom see the feet that made them,
walking away and
        away in patterns of loss.

To know the distance:
not to be a stranger to
loneliness
        and        emptiness
fallen from such a height.

# Cougar

Neighbors snorted
    but she clung to the majesty:
large cat, tan and buff,
    tail cleaves
cows in the meadow.

This cat knew his power;
he vanished as soon as appeared.
    She peered through the window; glass
did nothing to aid sight,
but gave her the courage of distance

which is where she is today:
three thousand miles
from the Laurentides where cougars
    are rare; here
they plop their paws in snow
and her house kittens
    mysteriously vanish.

Wild cat on cliff,
tail curved about his feet,
furred comma that makes the voice pause;
she listens through endless night
    for the single wrenching screech.

She listens for her own breath,
　　　her own speech,
but hears instead a whisper
she knows she'll follow,
　　　the purr
rubbing against every word—

Here! Here I
am! Hear
　　　my voice!
Squeeze between the stones,
　　　scramble up!

# Fry Creek

Cool, cool water giddy
over stone
splashes from the heights
where snow lingers in July
while we swelter below—
we can hardly hear
our own breaths
as the creek carves banks
deposits excess
makes a sandy point
where it enters the lake
and that's the point:
splash hushes chatter
so the deep reveals
its treasures, not counting
rocks or deciding
if this or that deserves
the soaking
and neither does grace
splashing in abundance;
we can be the rocks, we
can be the lake,
or shutting down
the sluice gate, we can
make the lake level drop—
we can even be
a desert.

# Ideas

We think of clouds as hardly there—
they have no ground,
evaporate,

and when you fly through them,
they wisp around
the plane, melt in the sky's mouth,

or rolling down the mountain,
they fog the lake
disguise the cliff,

but now they bang against each other
overhead—they
crackle and quake;

they might spark a tall tree
as energy seeks the ground and then

even the rain
        cannot put out the fire
they ignite.

# Drink

Drink up this sky
this froth of cloud.

Put your lips on the globe
of this rain.

Drop your thoughts
one per plop.

They'll ooze,
then let them bleed

Into this dry moment,
into the dusty memories.

Or better yet,
let them go.

They'll lift on the updraft;
you'll lose them,

You'll hardly notice,
but you'll see what they disguised.

# Rebar in Babel

Such a tower that rose,
stone by stone,
rebar, the bones of speech,
pushing further human reach

higher than the words of prayer,
higher than the edge of beach
where the limits used to be.

We know no limits now
but delve beneath the skin
and to the furthest end of the furthest sea
of stars and galaxies and ether;

deep beneath her
skin the sea yields up
oily blood
spurts fire—
        hell itself released;

and all is doubt and all
stirs us from sleep—
we'll catch on surely
before all's gone
but banks of stone,
the banks of sand now breached;

and yet the vowels and consonants
move our lips
trying to get it right:

your lips, as pink as the peaks at dawn
that bleed into the clouds;
your face, round and luminescent
as the moon;

but into that face
I can speak only silence

while words become keys that lock
        you and me
into the towers of our own tongue;

the words that come to my lips
bring down the shades in your eyes;
when I open my mouth to speak,

you already hear words I haven't said
and those I do say are little nuggets of sound
that sink into the pool of your expectation.

Our words are tied in knots;
even the words I know mean something else
in another mouth, mean something less
and something more.

The breath moves
into the locked places,
unraveling tangles,
under the crumbling mud
shaping the sounds that cross our lips;
something with the rigidity of steel
    holds true
underneath
    connecting us as one;

breathe the fire of new tongues
and find the word beneath the words
the strength that has been bent
    and dented;
find again the place we know
where logoi lurk.

# The Burgess Shale

The breathing, rumbling earth buckled up,
pushed the bottom of the sea to the highest mountain;

now rippling mountains remember rippling
Cambrian seas, and hikers finger marella and trilobites.

If I spoke the right word, if I gave you your true name,
would you rise like that? My stone heart

feels the breath of your words, softens like roses,
blushes slowly, pulsing to the very edges.
Already the earth's tomb has turned inside out.

New words spill drunkenly from our lips—

oh, this is not the wine that speaks,

this is fire dropping, like haloes, words in our own tongues;
water gurgling beneath the stones, a misty dew on my cheeks

sizzles against my stubborn will;
from sea to mountain, moistened with this new baptism

in rosy alpenglow,
we stand beneath the cliff; we climb.

# Struggle: A Jacob's Ladder

*Decayed branch sprouts*
*fungal trumpets;*

*what strange music*
*in the damp woods.*

We slip past a line of trees on the river bank,
feathery doubles glimmer and beneath the ground,
twice as large again, branches lift in orans, split

underground in secret prayer, infinitesimal
hairs curl up and over roots of nearby trees,
flutter messages, dendrite-like

through the mycelium: these
are the listening strands:
*We absorb each other's needs.*

We who are made from the same dust as trees,
we who breathe this air until we become this soil
                    move this way

        and that
through the stones in rising fog:
*We absorb desires that shatter.*

David of Thessaloniki in his tree,
hands extended, silence
an olive between his teeth,

chewed the demons and spit their pits
into the void as into a stream,
        into the water as river stones.

*We are made from living dust*
*and not the dust of demons:*
*We absorb desires that bind.*

The trees keep their place, even
when the wind creaks them.
They hold steady and show us our bearings.

They become our lighthouse. They become
the ladder linking sky to earth,
the ladder on which Life itself is pierced,

unraveling knots and knitting together the strands,
and the river rushing past
drags us along, rubbed clean and shining.

*Speak of roots that intertwine;*
*Speak of roots deep in the soil of time;*
*Root your speech in dreams and slime.*

Rumblings tug at the human mycelium:
there
        and also

here
we weave a web of hairs,
each seemingly insignificant;

        there, you act important;
here, I think and do not act;
we facilitate our deep undoing—

my choice, your snub, my hasty words
and each cut meshes underground entwining
what was said and what merely assumed

and how each step ensnares us,
wandering, no place to rest.

*Though closer than my next breath,*
*your words, your thoughts,*
*a torrent over me.*

Knock down one tree,
and the others silently scream;
knock down ten,

and the flood waters take the bank;
the hillside is ravished;

wipe out the forest,
and the animals slink into our yard
eat our kittens.

We stand straight as trees
and silent, linking arms beneath the soil
with our community, with the mushrooms

sprouting at our roots,
with the robins warbling from our branches.

*Wood is the life of our bones*
*and that on which our life hangs.*
*Wood we wear around our necks,*
*over our heads,*
*and under our feet.*
*Side by side, we stand erect,*
*sway under thewind's breath.*

Let the breath move through you—
breathe and hold on to the bark of the tree,
pick up your tiny branch and follow

the very steps that dance before you
up and down the ladder
up and down the tree

the piercing through of matter,
the life that rumbles through the roots
and surges up and up the channels

of desire we were meant for, the true
locus of all towards which we strive
and how it means to be
alive.

# Rhythm

Bring the words into your feet
tap them lightly
floor boards creak

Twirl around and feel the beat
lips slap sounds
down, up, soar sweet

Let the old heart's great ba boom
bounce around
the empty room

Take in breath then let it go
more and more
now fast, then slow

Small electrons spin around
ferns unfurl
planets turn round

Spinning suns in milky way
galaxies whirl
clusters sway

Fire within and fire without
dance in tandem
spin about.

# When the Wheel Turns

## I. Centrifugal Force

From the center, a casting outward: each generation
    a whoosh of spokes and rubber.

The great revolutions of Europe and America spin:
    Chopping heads,
they welcomed Napoleon whose golden resting place
    is more opulent than any king's;

The serfs found freedom, then Stalin strangled a nation;

Today American patriots
    would be locked away as terrorists.

I ride my bike down the driveway and into history.
    Air whips my face, exhilarates;
I depend on my own legs for power;
    my balance keeps me upright;
the initial surge up the hills
    —then I coast to the bottom and around the block.

All this turning and turning again:
    It is for something more I thirst.

It's not that outward changes don't matter;
    they chew on life and death
and often shatter bondage,
    and often steer the course of a spinning planet;

but just when it seems a new day patters along
      on stockinged feet,
that same old stone nudges up from the soil and trips me;
I cannot say my coat is tattered because of fine decisions;
I cannot say I haven't stumbled,

And simply in the saying mumbled some devastating loss
that came, not from over there,
      though I'd like to think it were the case,
but from here in my inner heart.

Still, one war rolls into another;
      wounds and hurt feelings fester, sprout boils
that ooze puss into the ground water.

## II. *Composting History*

With a few flicks, the beet peels sit blood red
       in my compost bucket,
cover the fuzz of sprouting potato skins
       and crushed egg shells.

I will toss the whole mess onto the garden pile
       where ravens will pick through it.
What's left will rot and sift into earth. I will turn it over
       and drop in seeds;
it will become beets again, blood red, staining my lips,
       your tongue.

I hold out my blood red hands and spin.

### III. Origami

On the west coast of Vancouver Island,
    beachcombers pick through debris
from a Japanese tsunami; for a year the flotsam
    bobbed on the Pacific waves,
got caught up by ocean current,
    washed up half a globe away.
Pink infant booties, a blue glass ball:
    shreds ripped from a life by waves of terror.

Unfold the structure and see our torn planet;
    look again at the patterns so lovingly formed.
These algorithms designed for beauty can solve problems,
    may someday save a life.
A heart stent folds into a water bomb; airbags fold up, too.

Take a sheet of paper;
make a crease pattern, a mathematical figuring of circles
    bent in mountains and valleys,

Like the eyeglass telescope, a football field in diameter;
fold the glass and send it into space;
    see into the future or the distant past;
the universe will watch us, watching.

### *IV.* *Centripetal Force*

My bike pulls me forward with the power of two legs spinning.
Neither winning nor rotting,
I seek the folds in the heart, feel my blood's waves thrash,
unfold new frames.

## You Are Meant to Be Like Fire

The satin sheen of this morning's lake
ruffled by a southern breath—
rain pocks the ripples, gathers force
of circles, then of wind.

Beneath the sheen of this moment
erupts the deep down fire,
deeper than that, a shift of the plate,
deeper still, the inner flame.

End days spurt into the present;
the rolling waves gain force—
and what happens across the planet
happens here.

Waves do not quench
the fire, and the wind whips it up—
and what happens under the ground of your heart
happens here.

# To a Glacier

*with thanks to Paul Walde's "Requiem for a Glacier"*

***Remembrance will be from generation to generation:
eternal memory***

We stand on your cold back
memories of ancient rock,
its thrust and buckling strength

holding moisture in cups
lifted in offering
where earth yearns for heaven.

You weep for our sins,
your tears a last gift to us
who cannot weep ourselves

roll off your cheeks in creeks
across your face,
life-giving waters stored, now released.

You are weeping for our sins:
we should be the ones weeping;
a true repentance turns things around
       —metanoia.

We are spared the total vision;
if we were to see ourselves as we really are,
we wouldn't be able to stop the tears,

but even seeing what we do see
necessitates a change.

Requiem sung to a glacier
as it oozes life:
we stand on frozen ground

hurling notes into the air;
the notes spike,
the mounting pressure,

the pure water
our lifeblood.
We gather to sing

dissonant notes, our voices
weave in and out—
who are we to sing this requiem

to such majesty?
Icy presence, storehouse of life for the planet,
sun and moon glow

on your purity,
crystal beauty,
rivulets on a stony cheek:

Beauty, O
beauty,
this harsh lament when

Glacier, you are not so different from us:
remote, hard to reach
yet sourcing life;

tears of the glacier
nearing the end
offering its last plea.
The earth weeps for our sins.

Listen, glacier,

stop for now your weeping:
we are singing,

our hearts are breaking,
these notes crystalize leaving
our mouths

and our lungs shiver;
the words we dare not speak
steam into the atmosphere;

we leak our carbon dioxide into the clouds.
You are weeping the tears we need
to weep with you;

instead, oily with greed,
we shoot poisoned water into the earth
for easy extraction of ancient treasure;

we shrug as if there's time to consider
those trees we cut down to improve the view,
that paper we crumpled,

those boards we split and threw
into the fire, those trees once sucked in
the poison we spewed,

but we thought there'd always be more sprouting up;
we didn't think it would matter
when as far as the eye can see

the boreal forest goes and goes;
and the tropical rain forest
is pruned back so we can grow more soybeans

so we can raise more beef;
but you exaggerate
it can't be as bad as all that,

you can't expect us to change
our lives that drastically;
still you weep,

still the dripping continues
and the bare rock nudges its chin
through its evaporating beard.

See, her bones lie
uneasy, in this dissolving beauty,
O beauty!

Strings shudder—
flutes pierce the air—
drums thunder against the mountain peaks.

We didn't come here just for an outing,
climbing the rocky back for a chance
to snow board in July;

we seek to deepen our connection,
to uncover the hidden hubris,
and we leave,
            weeping for our sins.